DARWIN'S ON LIFE SUPPORT!

A Brief Look At Replacing Darwinism

by: Malcolm Wayne Puckett, Ph.D.

Copyright Information

Darwin's on Life Support!
A Brief Look at Replacing Darwinism

By: Malcolm Wayne Puckett, Ph.D. ©2020

Published by:
Good News Fellowship Ministries
220 Sleepy Creek Rd.
Macon, Georgia 31210

ISBN-13: 978-1-7344999-6-4

Format by: Lisa Walters Buck

Table of Contents

Dedication and Acknowledgements

I dedicate this book to my readers who are seeking for truth about the origin of biological life, recognizing that it may have been hidden from them for many years. But facts are still facts, and truth is still truth.

I sincerely thank my wife, Aimee Michelle Andrews, for giving me space to write and supporting me with her ideas and comments. Others who helped with feedback include David M. Walters, Jason Cullum, Jennifer Nelson, and Owen Keith Puckett.

Overview

Charles Darwin's theory of biological evolution in <u>The Origin of Species</u> was published in 1859. The sparsity of physical evidence at that time made his theory of origins look possible, even reasonable. Since then, the physical evidence massively began to pile up, showing increasingly over time than his theory is not only disproven but that it is more like science fiction or fantasy than truth.

He has been so identified with his theory that it is as if he is still embodied in it. However, it is now over 160 years old and has taken so many hits from the negative evidence that it is essentially brain-dead and cannot survive on its own. In spite of that, its many powerful and vocal supporters are keeping it going through artificial life support, so to speak. We will take a high-level view at why this is true and at what is coming to take its place.

The Phenomenon of Intelligence

In looking deeper into this subject, note first the remarkably huge quantum leap (no transitional forms) from any of the animals to humans in the functioning of their minds. Mankind's ability to process information (learn and use laws of nature, make music, build complex machines, etc.) is phenomenally unique in nature.

Per Merriam-Webster online, these are some definitions of "intelligence":

- The ability to learn or understand or to deal with new or trying situations

- The skilled use of reason

- The ability to apply knowledge to manipulate one's environment or to think abstractly as measured by objective criteria (such as tests)

The animals who demonstrate the highest intelligence have severely restricted ability. Their limited communication ability can be enhanced somewhat by humans trying to teach them. Some can learn to understand up to 300-500 human words, which is nowhere close to the human ability to learn over 100,000 words that include abstract and intangible concepts. Mankind can develop tools and even classify them by type, from there creating huge machines and factories filled with exotic machinery. None of the animal species even come close.

The animals "closest to man" are the apes. In some studies, chimpanzees were taught how to do artistic oil painting. They became more skilled over time, developing beautiful symmetrical drawings that rivaled anything human. However, when the chimpanzees reached a certain stage, they became depressed, some even refusing to eat and dying from their depressed state. When comparing the development of chimpanzees to human babies, biologists discovered that the point at which a baby started drawing human forms was the point at which the chimpanzees became depressed. The chimpanzees did not have the self-awareness of human beings, and so they would hit a mental wall from which they could not recover.

This raises the question, "Why are humans so much more advanced in their minds than any of the animals?" They seem to be "god-like" in their ability to research and understand the mechanisms and operations of the world around them, and even of the farthest reaches of the universe.

Discovering What is True

To examine Darwinism properly, we have to establish how we discover what is true. The three realms for truth are the statistical, scientific, and detective.

<u>Statistics</u> examines random processes through personal experience to deduce recurring patterns. This is how we derived the bell curve of normal distribution and the entire realm of statistical analysis. This formed the basis of the laws of probability (or chance) that others can duplicate with the same results. Statistical analysis enables us to explain current events and predict the likelihood of future events.

<u>Science</u> is actually a subset of the statistical realm, mainly using The Scientific Method to put controls or restrictions on variables in a process to force the same exact results every time. For example, if we have two pair of dice with only one dot on each side, then the results will always be the number two. Science operates by forcing naturally random results into predictable patterns by human intervention. Science in its purest form enables us to establish controls on variables in normally random processes to force desired future results with a high degree of certainty.

<u>The Detective Process</u>, known and used primarily in the legal world, investigates evidence about past events, normally concerning an alleged crime. These events are not random but are static, fixed forever in the unchangeable past. Determining causes and effects is an inductive process, not a deductive scientific process. This type of analysis involves two primary kinds of evidence.

The first is human eyewitness testimony. Detectives search for credible humans who personally observed what happened. This requires the testimony of living humans for a recent event. For a distant past event, a "cold case," detectives examine written historical records for eyewitness accounts. In some cases, they may have to depend upon second-hand or third-hand accounts if that is all that is available. However, these are not as reliable as first-hand accounts where the witnesses prove to be trustworthy.

The second is forensics, which uses tools of science for examining physical evidence to form a picture or scenario of what most likely happened. Archaeology is thus a type of forensic research. Forensic experts use time stamps, location mapping, fingerprints, footprints, DNA evidence from hair and touched items, bones, tread marks, shreds of fabric, and so forth.

Finally, the detectives create possible space-time scenarios by combining the results of the testimonies and forensics. There may be several scenarios that develop, each with a different level of likelihood of occurrence. In many cases, the detectives seek further credible evidence until one scenario emerges as being by far the most likely either through a "preponderance of the evidence" or by being "beyond a reasonable doubt."

During this process, honest and ethical detectives begin with no presuppositions and are committed to "let the facts speak." It is critically important to examine ALL the evidence, not pick through the mass of facts to keep only those that support a desired outcome, ignoring the rest. For example, assuming that a bullet could not have caused a person's death would result in some twisted reasoning about how a small slug of lead ended up in the person's heart muscle. Further, there are many cases on record where ruling out a certain suspect led to a false conviction of someone else. This also applies to assuming only one suspect could have been the perpetrator, as with the Jon Benet Ramsey case where the father was thought to be guilty, but a criminal captured years later gave a voluntary credible confession to the crime.

Finally, after going through the fact-finding process, the detective team must choose the scenario that they believe best fits the facts. This decision or verdict is thus an act of faith, but not a blind leap since it is based upon a mass of credible evidence. The result may be surprising to many, but as Arthur Conan Doyle said through Sherlock Holmes, "When you have excluded the impossible, whatever remains, however improbable, must be the truth."

Commingling Realms of Truth

The major countering theory to Darwinism has been Creationism. I contend that the major area of confusion is the treatment of Darwinism as "science" and the other as only "religion." Instead, by both sides there has been a commingling of religion, cold case investigation, and true science in this critical area of the search for truth.

It must also be acknowledged that both theism and atheism are religious (and thus philosophical) concepts. Adherents to atheism will lean toward embracing a Darwinistic historical model, and theists will tend to lean toward embracing a Creationistic historical model. Unfortunately, both sides have not separated out their religious beliefs from the investigative process and conclusions.

Cold case investigation

In looking at the past, it is vitally important to see how the evidence aligns with one theory or another. The Bible and other ancient works should be treated as historical, rather than religious, for the purposes of determining what happened in the past. Therefore, they are valuable for developing theories of biological origins. The major theories thus fall into two major possibilities: 1) a random process based upon chance occurrences and 2) the intentional design and execution of a creator outside of the Universe. The evidence should be evaluated against both to see which best aligns with the evidence and which does not.

Science

The next step is to see how the <u>ongoing processes</u> can be studied by The Scientific Method. One aspect of The Scientific Method is to attempt to disprove competing hypotheses until only one remains. As it turns out, both the modern Darwinist and modern Creationist models align with the results of further scientific inquiry.

Religion

I believe this is where most of the confusion from commingling occurs. Adherents to Creationism often use the cold case results that point to a creator as a springboard to evangelizing others to belief in Jesus Christ. By doing this, they have undermined the legitimacy of their cold case analysis. On the other hand, atheists have done the same on the opposing side. However, they have carefully hidden their up-front atheistic bias that has driven their conclusions, especially in ignoring vast amounts of evidence that do not support their previously determined religious position.

What Do We "Know" About the Origins of Life?

Do we actually "know" anything about the origins of life? Everyone makes their way through this world by a combination of knowledge and belief. Most people have mistaken concepts about this, and so we must look next at the difference between knowledge and faith, what we can know versus what we believe.

Knowledge

We can only "know" what each of us personally experiences through our senses and which is then mentally processed into some form of understanding. Therefore, true knowledge is based only upon what each of us directly experiences through our senses.

And yet this is subject to misperception and false memory. For example, experimentation found that a class of college students might mistake a banana for a gun when someone broke into their class room and "shot" the professor. Strong emotions and past trauma can thus affect what we know and can remember of what we once knew.

Faith

Everyone lives by faith the great majority of the time. As in the detective process, we make verdicts and choices based upon credible evidence. As it is, most of our daily actions are based upon faith at every moment of choice. We sit in a chair because we believe it will support us. We drive along the road without fear because we believe the other drivers are keeping in their lanes and abiding by the laws. We eat our food believing that the cook is trying to give us a good meal and not harm us. We walk along paths believing that they will not have sink holes popping up to cause us to fall in. And so forth.

Case study

Do we "know" that man has been to the moon? I watched live on television as the first man set his foot on the moon. It dawned on me later that I did not "know" this for certain. What I saw on television could have been just a movie clip. Since I was not on the moon to have personal experience, I had to believe the people broadcasting the images. The only people who could "know" whether a man ever landed on the moon were the men who were on that mission. The rest of us, based upon extremely compelling evidence, must take what we saw and heard by faith.

Therefore, no living human can "know" anything about the past before their lifetime. This falls into the *detective realm of faith*, not the scientific realm of predictive knowledge. We use the tools of science for forensic research, but the process itself is not true science. Also, extant historical documents can present "eyewitness testimony," the other type of evidence examined by detectives.

Thus, theories of biological origins are <u>not science</u>!

They are inductions/verdicts about past events arising from <u>the detective process</u> that must be <u>accepted by faith</u>!

Focus of This Booklet

This booklet looks at biological life by setting aside the testimonial evidence (including in the Bible) and <u>focusing only on the forensic evidence</u>. Both Darwinism and Creationism are subject to the findings of this detective process, but we are focusing primarily on Darwinism here.

Darwin's Overall Concept

In Western civilization the prevailing view before Darwin was that God created everything as revealed in Genesis in the Bible. Charles Darwin first published his theory in 1859. In the 160+ years since then, most biological scientists still champion his overall theory, while setting aside major pieces of it and calling their current concepts Neo-Darwinism or by other names.

The basic concept of Darwin's theory of biological evolution is that more complex lifeforms "evolved" randomly from simpler life forms through natural selection without the involvement of an intelligent creator. Over time, the offspring had thousands of small inherited variations (mutations) that increased their ability to compete, survive, and reproduce (survival of the fittest). The simpler lifeforms supplied a launching pad from which the more complex lifeforms emerged.

Interestingly, a contemporary of Darwin was the hereditary scientist Gregor Mendel, who opposed Darwin's theory based upon his research and that of his contemporaries. The science of Genetics did not fully arise until the early 1900's, and most geneticists claim that Darwin's theory does not help explain genetics, based upon their experiments and research. Genetics is a true science in that its findings can be used to accurately predict future outcomes.

Darwin did not himself extrapolate back to the beginning of biological life, only postulating on how current higher forms came from lower forms. However, atheists and secular humanists wholeheartedly embraced his theory because it supported the views they already held. They extrapolated the concept into the past to include the origin of the first lifeform.

I have found that there are seven major requirements for proving the full scope of Darwin's theory as expanded by the others. The pieces of evidence necessary for analyzing these areas were mostly unknown and undiscovered in Darwin's time, and so his theory was certainly possible based upon the available facts at that time. However, in each of the seven requirements below, the mass of evidence accumulated in the last 160+ years has clearly shown that Darwinism and its offshoots have been disproven on every point.

The Forensics of the Seven Requirements of Darwinism

I believe there are <u>three show-stoppers</u> that invalidate Darwinism from the start. They are the existence of the laws of nature, the law of entropy, and the mathematical laws of chance and probability.

First, without a creator to make the laws of nature in the first place, how did the unthinking randomized Universe somehow "create" these complex laws by itself?

Next, the Second Law of Thermodynamics says that every action and reaction results in an increase of entropy, the loss of energy and reduced structural complexity. Thus, the concept of an upward evolutionary life process violates this fundamental law of nature.

Last, the mathematical laws of chance and probability show that the incredible complexity of biological life could never have happened by unthinking random acts of nature. We will take a brief look at just one of these complex biological molecules later on.

Just one of these three established truths is enough to discredit the entire Darwinistic model. Each will be discussed further in the following sections.

1. *NO CREATOR IS INVOLVED.*

This was an arbitrary position that was clearly a <u>false starting point</u> that prevented honest and ethical investigation from the start. His theory thus was already skewed and irrationally prejudiced. As we noted before, no credible professional detective rules out any possibility before gathering the evidence. Everyone is a suspect, and every conceivable cause is considered. Ruling out a major possible suspect or cause – intentionally - is the highest level of deception and treachery. Pursuing the detective process looking only for evidence that supports a forgone conclusion is outright fraud.

2. *INFINITE PAST TIME WAS AVAILABLE.*

Concept details

Darwin's theoretical processes required the Earth, and perhaps its biological system, to exist from eternity past, since it was assumed there was no creator. That meant the Universe also must have always existed. This vast amount of time would be required for the millions of mutations to allow so many thousands of higher lifeforms to arise and thrive. And there are roughly 30,000 identified species on Earth today.

Forensic evidence

Age of Earth and Moon. There are many indications that the Earth and Moon are only a few thousand years old. As an example, I remember that rocket scientists in the 1960's were concerned that the aged Moon might have around 20 feet thick of dust from millions of years of space dust build-up. But the dust layer is only about ¼ inch thick! This means the Moon is fairly young by astronomical standards.

For the Earth, the two main ways used to determine its age are radiometric dating and the fossil record within layers of sediment and rock deposited in the past.

First, radiometric dating assumes a uniform rate of decay of a radioactive isotope of carbon often present in lifeforms. However, this assumption of a uniform rate of decay cannot be proven; it is merely a "belief." Also, there have been numerous situations which show that radiometric dating is woefully inadequate. Therefore, when someone submits a sample of something for radiometric dating today, they must put on their form how old they think the sample is. Then by some magical process the operators of the radiometric machinery will prove that their estimate was essentially correct. This is a classic case of fraudulent circular reasoning.

Second, the same circular reasoning is used when dating items in sedimentary rock, the so-called "fossil record." Assuming vast amounts of time is just that: assumption. The fossil record cannot and does not prove that vast amounts of time were available.

Age of the Universe, or *Cosmos*. A major tenet of Darwin's theory as expanded by others was that the Universe and the Earth existed from eternity past. This vast amount of time was necessary for the millions of mutations eventually to evolve into the thousands of higher lifeforms randomly by pure chance.

However, the vast majority of modern astronomers agree that the Universe has not existed forever. Numerous observations show the Universe is expanding, and so the Universe was smaller in the past. Extrapolating back in time indicates the Universe would have somehow burst into existence from a tiny point. This gave rise to the Big Bang Theory. Estimating the age of the Universe under these concepts, and <u>assuming</u> a steady acceleration rate of expansion, has led to conclusions that the Universe is about 13.5-15 billion years old.

Interestingly, the concept of a six-day creation can be harmonized with the multi-billion-year concept. If the Universe has been expanding at nearly the speed of light, then anything <u>inside</u> the Universe would see little time change. But one observing from <u>outside</u> the Universe would see billions of years go by. This is the theme of the movie <u>The Genesis Code</u>.

If the Universe is indeed only a few billion years old, then the realities of statistical mathematics become a factor in determining how probable it was that something accidental and random would have occurred, especially something that is a "quantum leap" above the previous state. An example of this is given under the discussion of the seventh point on cell complexity, which mentions that one mathematician calculated the probability of a DNA molecule forming by chance is 1 in 10 to the 230th power, a number beyond comprehension.

The Big Bang Theory is appealing to theists, because it cries out for a creative agent to cause the original burst out of nothing, but it also has serious scientific issues. First, the angular momentum of spiral galaxies could not have been sustained for 13.5 billion years. Physicists have calculated that they could not be older than 0.5 billion years with their current shapes. Second, if the original atoms in the Universe were only hydrogen and helium, such as in stars, then the gases would have expanded rapidly outward and remained as gases. The gravitational forces needed to cause these gases to coalesce into stars and planets is far too weak. And there are issues with molecular structures in making more complex molecules from simpler ones.

Further, the Big Bang Theory cries out for an explanation for the very existence of the Laws of Nature. These must have been in place <u>before</u> the Universe began. Before the Big Bang or any other beginning point, the design parameters for the wonderfully <u>orderly way</u> the Universe would expand and operate must have been already in force, thus requiring a highly intelligent creator that was above nature, and thus supernatural. This point alone precludes a Universe governed only by mindless random actions as Darwinists believe.

Is there life elsewhere? In spite of the billions of planets that exist throughout the Universe, the probability is incomprehensibly low for another planet like Earth to be so perfectly fine-tuned for biological life. There are over 40 aspects of the Earth's extreme fine-tuning that have been identified as necessary for allowing and sustaining biological life. Among them are the circular orbit of the Earth around the sun at exactly the right radius, the perfect size and "age" of the Sun, and the large singular moon with a geosynchronous circular orbit at the exact distance away. And then to hope for the accidental appearance of the various biochemicals for spontaneous generation on such a finely tuned planet is even further beyond statistical possibility. Statistics cannot prove something is outright impossible, but reasonable doubt says probabilities such as 1 in 10 to the 230th power are beyond any believability.

3. *SPONTANEOUS GENERATION IS REAL.*

<u>Concept details</u>

Lifeforms like maggots were thought to spontaneously arise from rotting biological materials, and some microscopic lifeforms supposedly generated spontaneously from inanimate materials.

<u>Forensic evidence</u>

Most scientists in Darwin's time still believed in biological spontaneous generation. Aristotle had believed in it, and his ideas dominated until supplanted by Isaac Newton's laws of nature, which did not preclude the concept.

Nevertheless, there were a few early theorists debunking the concept of spontaneous generation, but their thinking was not generally accepted. Finally, Louis Pasteur published results of his research in 1858 that disproved the concept. He and others quickly showed that lifeforms only came from other lifeforms. Their pronouncement was, "Life begets life." Darwin was unaware of Pasteur's investigations, and spontaneous generation was a critical requirement for his expanded theory to be true. Ever since Pasteur over 160 years ago, it has been unquestionably affirmed within the general sciences, including biology, that there is simply no evidence for spontaneous generation. However, Darwinists cling to this as an article of faith because they must.

4. *MUTATION WAS AND IS THE PROCESS.*

Concept details

This is the one aspect of the theory that is amenable to The Scientific Method. There must be an ongoing mechanism that is capable of producing new - and higher – lifeforms.

Forensic evidence

To begin with, the ironclad Second Law of Thermodynamics destroys the entire concept of Darwinism in two ways. First, it destroys the argument that there could be a massive upward progression of lifeforms. This law states that in every chemical or physical reaction the measure of entropy, a concept of chaos, must increase. Therefore, going accidentally by random actions naturally from lower to higher forms that are sustainable is not possible, because the entire Universe is descending into simpler and more basic states. Second, since this law says the Universe is winding down and will one day be essentially dead, then if the Universe had existed from eternity past, it would already be in that depleted state.

Next, there are since 1859 records of many mutations that occurred within nature without human interference. Outside nature, we have similar records of the myriad of human experiments which forced mutations in laboratory settings. The key thing to note is that these many mutations were <u>always harmful</u> to the new lifeform. They never were more fit than their predecessors. There is evidence of minor short-term adaptations, such as the beaks of finches in the Galapagos Islands, but they are not on the deeper levels that Darwin's theory requires. Also, there is the case of the new species of finch on Galapagos which is impressive, but this is a parallel lifeform and certainly not a higher level one. In all such cases, the outcomes are readily explained by the laws of Genetics apart from Darwin's theory.

Finally, thousands of experiments have never shown the upward progress required of the mutation theory. Bats are fully bats. Fruit flies after dozens of generations of forced mutation are still fruit flies. There is "zero" laboratory evidence that higher lifeforms can "evolve" from lower lifeforms by an ongoing natural process. Further, humans are considered to be the highest lifeform with 23 pairs of DNA chromosomes, yet there are many animals and even plants with more than 23 pairs! Are they the truly "higher" lifeforms? Nonsense.

5. *MULTITUDES OF TRANSITIONAL FORMS WERE AND ARE THE FITTEST AND MOST SURVIVABLE.*

Concept details

In order for the upward evolutionary process to function, the newly arising lifeforms with their gradually more complex internal organs would have to prove to be more fit than the existing lifeforms, including in every one of their transitional forms. They must all survive and reproduce better than their immediate predecessor through thousands of minor changes to go from one major lifeform to another higher form. Darwin himself said,

> *If it could be demonstrated that any complex organ existed which could not possibly have been formed by numerous, successive, slight modifications, my theory would absolutely break down.*

However, He strongly believed that no such organs existed. He also admitted,

> *Our ignorance of the laws of variation is profound.*

In other words, he was strictly an observer of nature and was completely uninformed of the findings on hereditary traits that Mendel and others had been discovering.

Forensic evidence

The fossil record is a key area for finding evidence of transitional forms and is discussed in point 6 below. But other areas of evidence relate to this point.

First, embryology was once thought to be a help to the evolutionists, but it turns out that Ernst Haeckel's drawings used in textbooks after 1876 were not based upon reality. They were complete frauds, <u>misdrawn intentionally</u> to give the appearance of showing an evolutionary process, but detailed analysis has shown that embryonic development is significantly different from those drawings and offers no support for Darwinism.

Second, it was thought decades ago that the human body contains 180 vestigial organs that are no longer necessary, a "proof" of the evolutionary process. These included the appendix and tonsils. It has been demonstrated since then that all of these 180 organs provide useful functions, and so this "proof" has been eliminated entirely.

Third, arguing from the similarities between the various species does not prove that they evolved from each other. They all eat the same foods, they drink the same water, and they breathe the same air. Therefore, the biological processes in their bodies must be extraordinarily similar to each other for the whole ecological system to operate successfully.

Finally, we have the entire frenetic search for evidence of early man and "missing links" which is almost comical, if the stakes were not so incredibly high. Why this frenzied search? I believe their hopes and fantasies are shown metaphorically in the science fiction movie <u>Lucy</u>, which exposes the evolutionists' dream that mankind can become gods when fully energized or "evolved."

However, it is easy to note that all of the so-called "evidence" for early man can be placed on one office table. Outright hoaxes include Java Man, Australopithecus, Nebraska Man, and Piltdown Man. The last celebrated "discovery" was Richard Leakey's Lucy, based upon imaginative "reconstruction" and not legitimate detective procedures.

Along those lines, it has been shown that all of the <u>drawings</u> of early man from a few fragments of bone are just artists' conceptions based upon the assumptions of 1) great age and 2) apelike features, forcing the artists to go beyond proper professional reconstructive techniques. When reconstructive artists use the same bones, including those of "Lucy," to try and draw a <u>modern</u> person, they do so convincingly.

Finally, DNA scientists after extensive research have recently "found" that all humans and animals currently alive came from a single couple of their kind after some catastrophic event around 10,000 years ago. Their extensive evaluation of DNA evidence from animals worldwide forced them to acknowledge the likelihood of this unexpected conclusion.

6. THE FOSSIL RECORD <u>MUST</u> HELP PROVE THE THEORY.

<u>Concept details</u>

Fossils were known to exist all around the world, but no one had undertaken to make an intentional and comprehensive investigation of them. Darwin believed that more extensive study of the worldwide fossil records would by itself validate (or disprove) his theory by revealing thousands of transitional lifeforms.

<u>Forensic evidence</u>

Historically, there are ancient writings from around the world that mention an incredibly massive flood upon the Earth thousands of years ago. This explains well the geological finds we see today. If there was once such a massive worldwide flood, then the rock layers would have been formed all at the same time as the waters in the Earth moved around while the muddy floodwaters were receding. The dead plants and drowned creatures found in each layer or strata would be based upon the patterns of rapid sedimentation. Producing fossils and petrified plants in any layer requires laying their carcasses all at one time under dozens, maybe hundreds, of feet of mud and dirt to provide the necessary conditions for fossilization and petrification. The underground reserves of petroleum, natural gas, and coal would have been formed in the same way.

Instead, Darwinists have ignored the historical accounts in favor of assuming the fossils and petrified plants came from millions of years in the past. By <u>assuming</u> that the rock layers were formed over an extended period of time, the geologists can <u>believe</u> the rock layers were laid over millions of years. Then, sympathetic geologists named the assumed layers. In a classic case of circular logic, they give the age of a fossil based upon the layer it is in, and they date the age of the layer based upon the fossils that are in it. Geologists made hand-drawn charts that supposedly show the layers as they built up from the distant past. However, these drawings are not true representations of the rock layers actually found throughout the Earth. There is no place on Earth where all of these rock layers appear in the order shown. Some of the named rock layers are missing in many locations. And in other places the rock layers are in the wrong order, sometimes completely inverted. Yet you will seldom read anything about these disparities in Darwinist literature.

Along these lines, you will usually never read about the reality of "polystrate fossils." Evolutionary geologists refuse to acknowledge they exist. They speak disparagingly of the "Creationists" who use the term, but I have not seen any evolutionary geologist discuss them honestly. These are the many petrified trees which do not lie flat in any layer, but they lay at angles that cut through several geological layers. For a tree to petrify, it must be deeply and fully buried at one time. So how did a tree which was petrified at a single point in time come to penetrate several strata that supposedly formed over millions of years?

Next, since 1859, there have been hundreds of digs throughout the world for studying the fossils and the layers in which they are found. Although an occasional extinct species might appear to be a transitional lifeform, there is a remarkable and severe lack of the <u>multitudes</u> of transitional forms required by Darwin's mutative process, if there was such a viable process. There are huge gaps between the identified "ages," sometimes assumed to be as much as one billion years. In the so-called Cambrian age, there is a plethora of lifeforms that "suddenly" appear fully developed. This "sudden outburst" is preceded by a complete lack of transitional forms in the so-called Precambrian age.

Also, a number of particular situations profoundly frustrate the Darwinists. For example, there are no transitional forms seen from invertebrate to vertebrate lifeforms. The appearance of Placoderms frustrates them, along with several other similar "anomalies." The human eye, the hearing mechanism, and feathered wings are a few of the complex organs and systems that appear fully developed. And Darwinists are at a complete loss in showing how the male and female genders derived from genderless lower lifeforms.

The fossil record does <u>not</u> support Darwinian claims. It supports far better the results of massive universal flooding.

7. CELLS AND BIOLOGICAL COMPOUNDS ARE, AND MUST BE, SIMPLE IN STRUCTURE AND OPERATION.

<u>Concept details</u>

Cells and their chemical compounds had to be remarkably simple in their structure for Darwin's theory to be viable. Magnifying tools in Darwin's time could only show that cells existed, and that each had a little dot inside it, which they called the nucleus. They assumed each cell was a glob of a single homogeneous chemical, with a hard spot in the middle, and maybe a different chemical for the outer membrane. Therefore, it appeared that only three chemicals might be necessary to have a functioning cell. Biochemistry was in its infancy, and molecular structures of biological compounds were yet to be discovered.

<u>Forensic evidence</u>

This requirement is listed last because it took the longest time to have the tools necessary for full analysis. Sufficient magnification capabilities to the nano-level and below only came into being and extensive use since the mid-1990's, over 130 years after Darwin's theory was published.

First, cells have been shown to be fantastically complex in structure, far beyond what Darwin would have ever imagined, as exampled in the following figure.

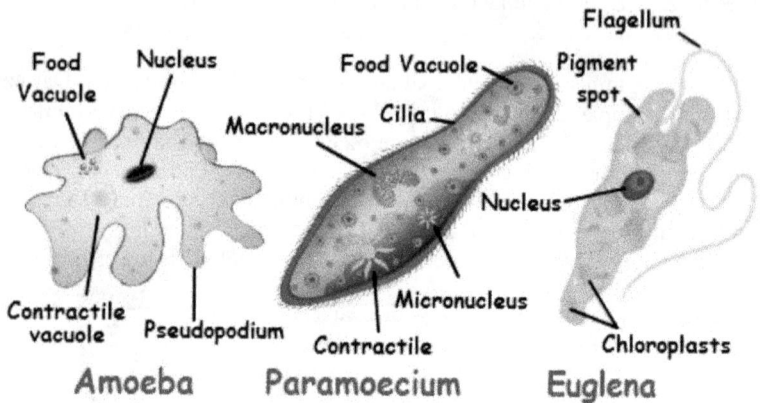

Figure 1. Three examples of single-cell organisms (From https://vivadifferences.com/difference-between-unicellular-and-multicellular-organisms-with-examples/)

This picture came from an article describing 15 major differences between unicellular and multicellular organisms. The single-cell organisms are marvelous in themselves, and yet the cells in higher lifeforms have over a dozen significant variations from these, further highlighting the reality of immense complexity in biological cells.

Second, every cell contains numerous different biochemicals, and these are the most complex naturally-occurring chemicals known to man. Major biochemicals include DNA, RNA, 21 amino acids that combine to make up roughly 30,000 different proteins, molecules that function as machines, and organic fluids that contain everything within each cell.

Third, the operations within every cell have been found to make up a tiny but remarkably complex "factory" with many molecular machines that fabricate and transport biochemicals to operate the many multi-stage processes required to capture food, ingest it, and then to eliminate the waste. They must also perform the complex process of reproduction. A fascinating example is shown here:

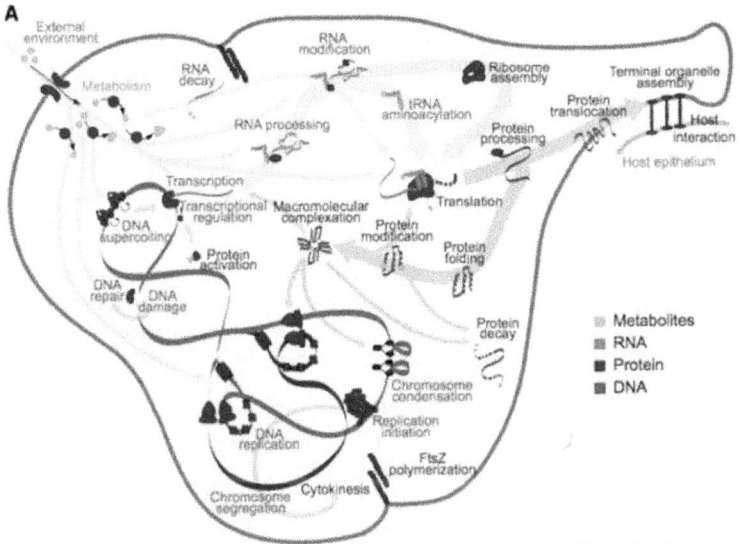

Figure 2. Example of the complex operations within the remarkable "factory" of a single cell. (From https://www. theatlantic.com/technology/archive/2012/07/to-model-the-simplest-microbe-in-the-world-you-need-128-comput-ers/260198/).

This cell that was analyzed using 128 high-powered computers over a long span of time is considered to be the "simplest microbe in the world." And yet there are at least 23 interrelated processes that are functioning concurrently inside of it. This is unimaginably greater than Darwin could have ever conceived, and yet it is demonstrably real.

Some of the other cell mechanisms that are astonishing include the flagella (and to some degree cilia) shown in Figure 1 that are complex machines with 40 distinct parts that must be constructed in a precise sequence. (And 30 of those parts are unique among biological components.) Our blood clotting mechanism and the operations of the immune system are fantastically elaborate. And these are just a few of the many incredible mechanisms in lifeforms. Watching the video series Unlocking the Mystery of Life demonstrates just how amazing the many cell operations are.

Fourth, take a closer look at just one of these many types of molecules, the marvelous DNA molecule. The structure of this molecule alone shatters Darwin's assumption of extreme simplicity. A typical DNA molecule is a spiraling double helix of 100's of millions of pairs of chemical bonds. It is so long that it exists in coils within coils. The length of the DNA in one human cell with its 3 billion pairs, if stretched all the way out, would be about 2 meters long. All the DNA in the cells of one human strung together would be twice the diameter of our Solar System!

All biological molecules, especially the DNA molecule, were unknown when Darwin published his theory in 1859. Gregor Mendel published his findings on hereditary traits in peas in 1866. Friedrich Miescher described the acidic substance in cell nuclei in 1869, calling it nuclein, which was later named DNA. It was not until 1911 that Thomas Hunt Morgan demonstrated that genes are located linearly along the chromosomes in DNA. And it was only after 1950 that scientists began to understand the actual structure of DNA molecules. Mapping the human genome was not completed until 2003.

The amazing thing about the DNA molecule is that only in recent decades did scientists determine that the millions of pairs in the molecules are a coded set of messages. Codes are a complex form of language for "information processing," and complex language is vested in only the highest of biological beings, humans. This shouts that there was an intelligent being outside of and beyond nature that established the information processing system in every biological cell.

One statistician has estimated that the likelihood that a DNA molecule could be formed by accident is one in 10 to the 230th power. This is an unimaginably high number. Considering that the number of carbon atoms in the Universe may be around 10 to the 46th power helps us to see how impossible it is for even just one DNA molecule to happen randomly by accident.

Human imagination is so powerful that we can conceive of many things that are impossible. And yet the hard realities of statistical probability cannot be overcome when dealing with actual occurrences in the very real space-time Universe. Consider the probability of flipping a balanced coin in an ideal random environment and getting heads every time. The chance of having 10 straight head flips is 1 in 2 to the 10th power, or 1 in 1,024. This seems like it should be easy to accomplish, but 1 in 1,024 is shocking. And that is only for 10 flips! Rounding 1,024 to 1,000 shows the probability of heads in 20 straight flips is 1 in 1 million, for 30 straight heads it is 1 in 1 billion, and for 40 straight heads it is 1 in 1 trillion, etc. Humans can imagine flipping only heads for hundreds of times, yet the real chance or probability of this actually ever happening is shockingly infinitesimal.

Thus, although Darwinists can conceive of many things "happening by chance," the laws of probability destroy their fantasies. What is the probability of two strings of DNA forming by accident (each with a 1 in 10 to the 230th power chance of occurring independently) to form a pair, along with the 21 amino acids, and the numerous other features and chemicals in a single-celled organism all coming together within a surrounding membrane by random actions, with the DNA molecule acting as the code for at least 23 different processes to occur within the cell, including its ability to reproduce? And yet they continue to say, "Well, we know this is what happened!"

Final Verdict on the Claims of Darwinism

- Making any assumptions before the evidence is carefully analyzed is a deceptive and thus <u>false</u> starting point.

- Most scientists now accept that the Universe is no more than 13.5-16 billion years old. The assumption of an infinitely old universe needed for the vast number of mutations is <u>false</u>.

- Spontaneous generation has been demonstratively <u>disproven</u>.

- Through the plethora of unsuccessful science experiments, the concept of mutation developing higher lifeforms has been soundly <u>disproven</u>.

- The "data" for the many transitional forms from the supposed mutative process through such related concepts as vestigial organs and embryology have proven to be mere science fiction, fantasies illustrated in fraudulent drawings. The remarkable lack of credible evidence for the numerous transitional forms that are required demonstrates that the concept of multitudinous transitional forms is <u>false</u>.

- The fossil record's a) severe lack of evidence for transitional forms along with b) numerous counterindications reveal that the mutative process for developing higher lifeforms is <u>disproven</u>.

- Cells and biological compounds are staggeringly complex, proving that Darwin's prerequisite of extreme cell simplicity is <u>false</u>.

Seven necessities for Darwinian evolution. ALL heavily disproven, thus demonstrating convincingly that the entire theory is …

<u>FALSE!!!!</u>

Intelligent Design Gaining Momentum

The most recent countering theory, other than Creationism, to Darwinism is Intelligent Design (ID). Darwinists insist that this is Creationism in new clothes, but that is an outright lie. It does not start with historical documents. It responds to the massive amounts of forensic data that have overthrown Darwinism to produce the most reasonable explanation, ala Sherlock Holmes. Many of the ID proponents began as committed and unquestioning Darwinists.

Looking at the mass of evidence available today, a reasonable person would see that there must be some incredible intelligence outside the universe. The Cosmos and biological life on Earth scream of construction by vastly intelligent intention, of intervention by "Design!" It is the only logical alternative to "accident."

Remember that Darwin said that his theory would break down if it could be shown "that any complex organ existed which could not possibly have been formed by numerous, successive, slight modifications." Over 160 years ago, the necessary data on the composition of organs was nonexistent. Now the data is readily available, and so a primary concept of ID is "irreducible complexity" in such things as the flagella and cilia in single-celled animals, the gaseous explosions of bombardier beetles, the human eye, the human ear, and more. If a complex organ or mechanism cannot be reduced in complexity to allow incremental steps of development, then it must have first appeared in a fully formed state, and this cries out for a preexistent designer-builder that is super-intelligent and immensely powerful.

The theoretical viewpoint of ID is in its infancy, and it is being fought ferociously by the entrenched Darwinists. A leading proponent is Michael Behe, and I encourage the reader to look into his writings and others in the ID genre.

How Do We Explain the Entrenched Faith in Darwinism?

Why is it that the vast majority of persons with college degrees, especially those with doctorates, all assert that Darwinism is de facto the whole truth about the origins of biological life which should be accepted by everyone? There are several factors in play here.

Misclassifying the area of truth-finding

The most glaring issue is classifying Darwinism as "science" and Creationism as "religion." When looking at past events, they both are cold case investigations which should be analyzed by the methods of the detective process. This false distinction has led to massive misunderstandings and false evaluations of the facts, both from forensics and from historical records. There are a few areas of modern Darwinism and modern Creationism that are amenable to The Scientific Method (See Jeanson's Replacing Darwin), but everything that happened in the past can properly be examined only by detective methodology.

Therefore, aside from forensics, written accounts from the past should be considered as forms of "eyewitness testimony." However, most Darwinistic investigators refuse to consider this second area of detective evidence, insisting that all of the applicable evidence predates written history, thus allowing them to examine only the physical evidence of their choosing. This restricted use of forensics allows them to support the inferences and conclusions they need to hold onto their philosophical worldview of atheism.

Indoctrination and selective ignorance

All graduates of public high schools and universities are subjected to many hours of indoctrination in Darwinism without exposure to available countering views. Most college students at all levels never study any of the claims of Creationism (or even ID). They take Darwinism as an article of faith without knowing anything about the vast amount of evidence against it. Creationists study the views of their opponents, but Darwinists do not. Therefore, it is easy for Darwinists to believe they have the only truth. They are ignorant of any other opposing viewpoint.

Creationist evangelism

There is a huge amount of evidence that successfully discredits Darwinism in Creationist literature. However, Creationists have historically used their writings as a way to end their presentations with a segue immediately into proselytizing for Christianity. They present a marvelous technical scenario where numerous pieces of evidence support there being a creator as a more reasonable scenario than that the Universe operates by blind random chance. But then at the end of their writings they jump into promoting the Bible as the Creator's revelation of who he is and challenge the reader to embrace Jesus Christ as Lord and Savior. This effectively delegitimizes their earlier presentation of credible evidence by switching to religious appeals at the end.

Virtual reality

In our day, forms of virtual reality are preferred by multitudes in developed countries over interactions in the real world. Science fiction is a major avenue for mental escape from daily life, with people preferring to live in an online virtual reality being the theme of movies like <u>Surrogate</u> and <u>2047</u>, among others. We have cosplay, online role play games, and other forms of fantasy. Many spend more time gaming, texting, and posting online than relating to other people face to face. And we know from psychology that the mechanism of denial of reality is powerfully active in many people all around us.

This is partially how we explain the attitude of "absolute certainty" that atheists such as Richard Dawkins claim they have for Darwinism. There is a flaw in human nature that causes us to miss important things that are happening because we are focused on some other particular thing. I watched a video once in a class where we were told to watch young people in a circle bouncing a basketball to each other. We were told to count the number of bounces in the one-minute clip. Most of us got the number of bounces correct. However, we missed the fact that a person in a black gorilla suit walked through the group as they were bouncing the ball. None of us saw that, but we could clearly see it when it was replayed for us.

This is where the atheists have missed the truth. They are so convinced that there is no God that they only see the evidence that supports their belief. They are blind to the many statistical impossibilities and the numerous pieces of evidence of irreducible complexity that scream for an intelligent creator, because these clearly shatter their paradigm and its underlying worldview. Therefore, they hold onto Darwinism tenaciously because they must, not because it is true. In our time, when there is such a mass of evidence disproving their precious paradigm, they are forced to continue believing it by blind faith. Their attitude is, "Don't confuse me with the facts. I've already made up my mind."

Arguing from authority and paradigm shifts

A major argument of Darwinists is that hundreds of prominent scientists have gone on record as agreeing to the same theory about past events, yet this proves nothing whatsoever. The great body of scientists once believed that the Earth was flat and that the sun revolved around the Earth. Now the majority agree on their belief in something else. **Truth is not determined by voting**! Ironically, some of the people who call themselves evolutionists are starting to lament the dogmatism that they find inside their own profession.

All of the major scientific theories have changed over time. The culture of the insiders in any profession has always resisted innovative ideas. Note the furor over Einstein's theories as they expanded the concepts of Newtonian Physics. And Newtonian Physics superseded the system of analogous constructs of Aristotle that had been accepted without question for hundreds of years before that. Thomas Kuhn calls this phenomenon of changing major viewpoints within a profession a "paradigm shift." What we are witnessing today is a serious paradigm shift from Darwinian Evolution to Intelligent Design.

Conclusion

Whatever you call it, Darwinism or Neo-Darwinism or just Evolution, the basics of that theory are categorically <u>not</u> supported by the preponderance of the forensic evidence gathered in the last 160+ years, and especially in the last 20+ years. Yet its defenders and proponents are woefully ignorant of such evidence, trusting by blind faith in the slanted indoctrination that they have received. It is well past the time when everyone should call out, "Time's up! Darwin failed!" The longer we keep looking, the more the evidence <u>against</u> Darwinism continues to pile up. The false Darwinian paradigm is the religion of atheism (or pantheism) disguised as science, and Intelligent Design is arising as the new paradigm to supersede it.

Dr. Chandra Wickramasinghe says,

> *The speculations of The Origin of Species turned out to be wrong.*

And S. Lovtrup has asserted,

> *I believe that one day the Darwinian myth will be ranked as the greatest deceit in the history of science. When this happens, many people will pose the question: "How did this ever happen?"*

As discussed earlier, the two tools of the detective process are 1) forensics and 2) testimony. Since <u>the forensic evidence destroys Darwinism</u> and shouts that there certainly <u>must be</u> an intelligent Creator of some kind, the next question is, "What does the testimony of history tell us about a creator?" The ensuing search leads to a study of historical documents to see if the Creator has revealed anything of its nature to mankind. And what can we determine from those records? If we honestly investigate as researchers like C. S. Lewis and Lee Strobel did, then honest men and women will find the God of the Judeo-Christian Bible.

Brief Bibliography: Suggested Resources for Deeper Study

There are numerous excellent publications on this topic. A sampling is listed below.

My Favorite:

Wells, Jonathan. *The Politically Incorrect Guide to Darwinism and Intelligent Design*

Other websites and publications:

Documentary: *Unlocking the Mystery of Life* from Illustra Media

Movie: *The Genesis Code*, released in 2010.

https://darwinanddesign.com

https://discovery.org

https://nypost.com/2018/11/24/turns-out-all-of-humanity-is-related-to-a-single-couple/

Behe, Michael J. *Darwin's Black Box: The Biochemical Challenge to Evolution*

Bergman, Jerry. *Evolution's Blunders, Frauds and Forgeries*

Demski, William A. *The Design Revolution: Answering the Toughest Questions about Intelligent Design*

Gills, James P., and Tom Woodward. *Darwinism under the Microscope: How Recent Scientific Evidence Points to Divine Design*

Gish, Duane T. *Evidence against Evolution*

Gish, Duane T. *The Amazing Story of Creation*

Ham, Ken. *The Lie*

Jeanson, Nathaniel T. *Replacing Darwin*

Johnson, Phillip E. *Darwin on Trial*

Johnson, Phillip E. *Defeating Darwinism by Opening Minds*

Kuhn, Thomas. *The Structure of Scientific Revolution*

Meyer, Stephen C. *Signature in the Cell, DNA, and the Evidence for Intelligent Design*